WHAT IS TAO?

WHAT IS TAO?

ALAN WATTS

NEW WORLD LIBRARY
NOVATO, CALIFORNIA

New World Library
14 Pamaron Way
Novato, California 94949

Editors: Mark Watts, Marc Allen
Cover design: Mary Ann Casler
Text design: Tona Pearce Myers
Interior Calligraphy: Alan Watts

Library of Congress Cataloging-in-Publication Data

Watts, Alan, 1915–1973.
What is Tao? / Alan Watts.
p.   cm.
ISBN 1-57731-168-X
1. Tao. I. Title.

B127.T3 W39 2000
299'.514—dc21   00-056091

First printing, October 2000
ISBN 978-1-57731-168-3
Printed in Canada on 100% postconsumer-waste recycled paper

10   9   8   7   6   5   4   3   2

The tao that can be told
is not the eternal Tao.
The name that can be named
is not the eternal Name.

The unnameable is the eternally real.
Naming is the origin
of all particular things.

Free from desire, you realize the mystery.
Caught in desire, you see
only the manifestations.

CONTENTS

INTRODUCTION

By Mark Watts

The ancient philosophy of the Tao is one of the most intriguing and refreshing ways of liberation to arrive in the West from the Far East in modern times. With over fifty translations of the *Tao Te Ching* into Western languages to date, the classic work of Taoist literature offers its readers great wisdom for living as well as advice on worldly affairs. It is also a fascinating window into the mysterious world of pre-dynastic China.

The very practical nature of Taoist thought is often overlooked by Western readers who are hesitant to embrace a seemingly strange and foreign way of knowing, but in the philosophy of the Tao one finds a surprisingly contemporary perspective. The word *Tao*, properly pronounced "dow," has lent its name to a way of understanding and living in the world with profound implications for modern societies. Above all else Taoism places great emphasis on the balance between our human awareness and our natural being, as an integral part of the web of life. It embodies our deepest understanding of ecological awareness.

The mystical side of Taoist thought, on the other hand, is highly enigmatic, for here one finds a doorway into the shamanistic world that flourished in China over a span of at least five thousand years, right up to the period in which the Taoist texts were written.

As Alan Watts explains it, the word Tao embodies two broad meanings in our language: it means approximately the Way — in the sense of "the way to go" — and it also refers to nature in the sense of one's own true nature. Everything is said to have its own Tao, but it is impossible to define it, to put one's finger on it exactly.

As I sat working on this manuscript my eight-year-old son came up to me and asked, "Papa, what are you working on?" I told him it was a book on the Tao, and began to explain a little bit about it, but without a moment's hesitation he said, "Oh, you mean what's behind everything" — and then he headed off. Intuitively and experientially we know what it is, but for most of us the problem arises when we try to explain it.

This enigma reminds me of a story that my father used to tell about a debate years ago in the House of Lords in England concerning a Church-related matter. Apparently one of the representatives had put forth the argument that it was not proper for a governing body with so many atheists to rule on a religious issue. One of the members rose to the occasion, however, and replied, "Rubbish, Sir! I am quite certain that everyone here believes in some sort of something somewhere or other." And by and large we do even if it is no more definite than to sense the Tao.

In classic Chinese literature the Tao is described as following the path of least resistance, occupying the invisible or lowest position, and embracing the goodness of nature without ever attempting to do so. The Tao is passive but not weak, and in his book the legendary sage Lao-tzu describes the paradoxical quality of the Tao by asking one to consider the following:

> *How do coves and oceans become kings of the hundred rivers?*
> *Because they are good at keeping low —*
> *That is how they are kings of the hundred rivers.*
> *Nothing in the world is weaker than water,*
> *But it has no better in overcoming the hard.*

THE ORIGIN OF THE TAO TE CHING

The *Tao Te Ching* has traditionally been attributed to Lao-tzu, the legendary sage and founder of the Taoist school. However, the *Tao Te Ching* was originally called the *Lao-tzu* as well, and this makes it difficult for us to fully understand the origin of the earliest texts describing its origin because in

Chinese it is often impossible to know whether "Lao-tzu" refers to the person or the text. Nevertheless the original work has been tentatively dated to the sixth century B.C.E., the time in which Lao-tzu was supposed to have lived, although it is likely that the collection did not come into circulation until the fourth century B.C.E. This was the period of the golden age of Chinese philosophy that gave rise to tremendous diversity — known as "the hundred schools" of thought — and gave us the other great classic of Chinese literature, the *I Ching*.

It is not until the first century B.C.E., however, that we find a history, the *Shih chi* (or *Records of the Historian*), that contains one of the oldest recorded stories about Lao-tzu. Here we find the story of Confucius visiting Lao-tzu at the Court of Chou where, by this account, Lao-tzu served as the court librarian. In that meeting, Lao-tzu was said to have scolded Confucius for his pompous and self-serving ways, and afterward Confucius is reported to have said to his disciples:

"I know that birds can fly, fish can swim, and animals run. For those that run a net may be set, for those that swim a line cast, and for those that fly an arrow set free. But a dragon's ascent to heaven walks the wind and swims through clouds, and I know of no way to trap him. Today I have met Lao-tzu, who is both man and dragon."

The reference to the ascension of the dragon to heaven offers a clue to the early origins of Taoist rituals, because it reveals a link to the ancient shamanic ancestry of the region. The dragon, like the Feathered Serpent in South and Central American mythology, combines the scales of the snake with the feathers or wings of the bird. The feathers or wings of the dragon or bird are representative of the shaman's flight, and the scales represent rebirth, for the snake sheds its skin only to find a new one beneath the old.

The combination of these attributes accurately describes dream/death and rebirth rituals of the shamans known to date far back into the Neolithic period. Pottery dating from 5000 B.C.E. discovered in the village of Banpo near Xi'an in the 1950s included a ritualistic vessel showing four views of a shaman in a dreaming or trance state, and a fifth as a transformed being. This pottery example is fairly typical of representations of the wizards who were said to leave their bodies in flights of vision, and following such a flight the shaman or initiate would be reborn with the sunrise fully transformed.

Although the antiquity of the underpinning is apparent, the actual history of the legendary sage Lao-tzu has proved to be elusive. To further obscure matters, the histories we do have that mention Lao-tzu were not recorded until hundreds of years after the events they detail, and it is possible that some of the facts were adapted to corroborate the legendary accounts of the origin of his works.

One popular legend holds that the *Tao Te Ching* was written in the gatehouse by Lao-tzu as he was about to leave his post in the city to retire and become a hermit in the country. According to this story the gatekeeper is said to have insisted that Lao-tzu record his wisdom before he left. Another more plausible theory is that the philosophy was recorded over a period of time by several anonymous writers to give the benefit of the country dwellers' wisdom to the rulers of the cities, in the hope they would make life easier for the common people — and the gatehouse story may simply be symbolic of the source of this knowledge originating outside the pale. This theory fits in with the tumultuous climate of the Warring States period, and is supported by the fact that the later chapters of the work carry decidedly political overtones and candidly offer advice to those in positions of authority.

In the first century A.D. the *Lao-tzu* was divided into two works, and so we received the *Tao Ching* and the *Te Ching*. This division reflects the varying emphasis of each section of the book, the first on the Tao and the second on *Te*, which means approximately "virtue," though Alan Watts calls it "skill at living." These sections were then combined to form the book we know today.

Some scholars firmly believe the *Tao Te Ching* is in fact a compilation of writings by various authors who simply attributed their works to the legendary Lao-tzu; however, the consistency of the style and the rhythm of the arguments presented in both parts of the work suggest otherwise. It seems more likely that this book of sage advice was the work of a single author drawing upon the prevailing folk wisdom of his day, and that perhaps the two books were written during different periods of the author's life, or in response to different issues.

THE PHILOSOPHY OF NATURE

Taoism has often been described as the philosophy of nature, and it is in this respect that its wisdom most strongly suggests its origins were in the shamanic world of pre-Dynastic China. Living close to the earth one sees the wisdom of not interfering with the course of life, and of letting things go their way. This is the wisdom that also tells us not to get in our own way, and to paddle with the current, split wood along the grain, and seek to understand the inner workings of our nature instead of trying to change it.

According to the laws of nature every creature finds its own way, and so each of us is known to have our own path or way. In classic Chinese texts there are references to the Tao of Earth with all its creatures, the Tao of Man, which refers to our awakened path, and to the Tao of Heaven, by which the broad forces of heaven and earth come together in a field of polar energies. Together these forces create the world in which all life plays, and instill in us the instinctive knowledge of the primal forces at work in the human psyche.

In this book, Alan Watts brings his years of study of the Tao into focus through lively explanations of the essential ideas and terms of Taoist thought. He gives the reader an opportunity to experience the Tao as a personal practice of liberation free from the limitations of the commonly held beliefs within our culture. This book is based on talks given during seminars during the last ten years of his life, and it offers a way of understanding the true value of ourselves as free-willed individuals enfolded within the ever-changing patterns of the natural world.

We explore the wisdom of the way things are of themselves (*tzu-jan*, or "by itself so"), and of letting life unfold without interference and without forc-ing matters when the time is not right *(wu wei,* or "not forcing"). In the philosophy of the Tao we soon discover that striving to succeed — in the theory that "you can't get something for nothing" — must be balanced by the realization that "you can't have something without nothing," because something always requires its opposite, a place to be, whether it is a receptive vessel, a clear mind, or an open heart.

PART I

THE WAY
OF THE TAO

When people see some things as beautiful,
other things become ugly.
When people see some things as good,
other things become bad.

Being and non-being create each other.
Difficult and easy support each other.
Long and short define each other.
High and low depend on each other.
Before and after follow each other.

Therefore the Master
acts without doing anything
and teaches without saying anything.

OUR PLACE IN NATURE

Many years ago, when I was only about fourteen years old, I first saw landscape paintings from the Far East. It was as a result of looking at these paintings that I first became interested in Eastern philosophy. What grasped me and excited me about the Asian vision of the world was their astonishing sympathy and feeling for the world of nature.

One painting in particular that I remember was called *Mountain after Rain.* It showed the mist and clouds drifting away after a night of pouring rain, and it somehow pulled me into it and made me feel part of that mountain scene. It is fascinating for us to consider that pictures of this kind are not just what we would describe as landscape paintings, because they are also icons, a kind of religious or philosophical painting.

In the West, when we think of iconographic or religious paintings, we are accustomed to pictures of divine human figures and of angels and saints. When the mind of the Far East expresses its religious feeling, however, it finds appropriate imagery in the objects of nature, and in this very important respect their feeling for nature is different from ours. The contrast in these two forms of expression arises as a result of the sensation that the human being is not someone who stands apart from nature and looks at it from the outside, but instead is an integral part of it. Instead of dominating nature, human beings fit right into it and feel perfectly at home.

In the West our attitude is strangely different, and we constantly use a phrase that sounds peculiar indeed in the ears of a Chinese person: We speak of "the conquest of nature" or "the conquest of space," and of the "conquest" of great mountains like Everest. And one might very well ask us, "What on Earth is the matter with you? Why must you feel as if you are in a fight with your environment all the time? Aren't you grateful to the mountain that it lifted you up as you climbed to the top of it? Aren't you grateful to space that it opens itself up for you so you can travel right through it? Why do you even think of getting into a fight with it?"

Indeed, it is this domineering feeling that underlies the way we use technology. We use the powers of electricity and the strength of steel to carry on a battle with our external world, and instead of trying to live with the curvature of the land we flatten it with bulldozers, and constantly try to beat our surroundings into submission.

The problem is that we have been brought up in a religious and philosophical tradition that, to a great extent, has taught us to mistrust the nature that surrounds us, and to mistrust ourselves as well. We have inherited a doctrine of original sin, which tells us not to be too friendly, and to be very cautious of our own human nature. It has taught us that as reasoning and willing beings we should be suspect of our animal and instinctual nature.

In one sense this is all very well, for we have indeed achieved great technological advances through harnessing the powers of nature. If we carry this effort beyond a certain point, however, our manipulations interfere with the very course of nature, and this gets us into serious trouble indeed.

As a result of our interference we are experiencing today what we could call the "law of diminishing returns." For example, we want to go faster and faster everywhere we go, and so we attempt to obliterate the distance between ourselves and the place we are trying to reach. But as the result of this attempt to minimize the span of the Earth between these points, two things begin to happen.

First, all places that become closer and closer to each other by the use of jet planes tend to become the same place. The faster you can get from Los Angeles to Hawaii, the more Hawaii becomes exactly like Los Angeles. This is why the tourists keep asking, "Has it been spoiled yet?" What they are really asking is, "Is it just like home?"

Second, if we begin to think about our goals in life

as destinations, as points to which we must arrive, this thinking begins to cut out all that makes a point worth having. It is as if instead of giving you a full banana to eat, I gave you just the two tiny ends of the banana — and that would not be, in any sense, a satisfactory meal. But as we fight our environment in our tendency to get rid of the limitations of time and space, and try to make the world a more convenient place to live, this is exactly what happens.

For a much better understanding of our place in nature, we can look to the great religions and philosophies that blossomed and took deep root in the consciousness of so much of the population throughout Asia and the Far East.

TAOISM AND CONFUCIANISM

There are two great main currents in traditional Chinese thinking: the Taoist current and the Confucian. Both of them agree on one fundamental principle, and that is that the natural world in which we live, and human nature itself, must be trusted. They would say of a person who cannot trust his own basic nature, "If you cannot trust your own nature, how can you trust your own mistrusting of it? How do you know that your mistrust is not wrong as well?" If you do not trust your own nature, you become as tangled up as anyone can be.

Their idea of nature is that which happens of itself so, and that is a process which is not fundamentally under our control. By definition it is that which is happening all on its own, just as our breathing is happening all on its own, and just as our heart is beating all on its own — and the fundamental wisdom behind Taoist philosophy is that this "self-so" process is to be trusted.

Taoist thought is generally attributed to Lao-tzu, who is thought to have lived somewhere around 400 B.C.E., and to Chuang-tse, who lived from 369 to 286 B.C.E. Taoism is known to us as the uniquely Chinese way of thought, living, and liberation, although its roots certainly lie in shamanic traditions common to much of northeastern Asia, and probably to North America as well. In its final form, however, it is so similar to Buddhism that Taoist terms are often used to translate Sanskrit texts into Chinese. Once Buddhism was imported to China, Taoism so completely permeated Mahayana Buddhism in general and Zen Buddhism in particular that the philosophies of these schools are often indistinguishable.

Like Vedanta and yoga in India, older gentlemen in China traditionally adopted Taoism after they had made their contribution to society, and thereafter they would retire to primitive dwellings or caves to live in the wild and meditate for long periods of time. As in Buddhist lore, where the return of the sage into the world is known as the path of the Bodhisattva, Taoist stories are filled with accounts of the return of the liberated sage into worldly affairs. In fact the primary text, the *Tao Te Ching*, was originally written as a manual of advice for the ruling class. The teachings of Lao-tzu and of Chuang-tse must not be confused, incidentally, with the Taoist cult of alchemy and magic preoccupied with life extension — that is Taoist only in name, and not in practice.

Although Taoism proper has never become an organized religion, it has attracted the curiosity of scholars and philosophers of the Far East for more than two thousand years.

Taoism regards the entire natural world as the operation of the Tao, a process that defies intellectual comprehension. The experience of the Tao cannot be obtained through any preordained method, although those who seek it often cultivate inner calm through the silent contemplation of nature. Taoists understand the practice of *wu wei*, the attribute of not forcing or grasping, and recognize that human nature — like all nature — is *tzu-jan*, or "of-itself-so."

When we look to Confucian ideas, which governed Chinese moral and social life, we find a different word that represents the basis of human nature. This word has a funny pronunciation, and although we Romanize this word in English as *jen*, it is pronounced "wren," with a sort of rolling "r." This word is symbolic of mankind's cardinal virtue in the system of Confucian morality, and it is usually translated "human-heartedness" or "humanness." When Confucius was asked to give a precise definition of it, though, he refused. He said, "You have to feel the meaning of this virtue. You must never put it into words."

The wisdom of his attitude toward defining *jen* is simply that a human being will always be greater than anything they can say about themselves, and anything they can think about themselves. If we formulate ideas about our own nature, about how our own minds and emotions work, those ideas are always going to be qualitatively inferior — that is to say, far less complicated and far less alive —than the actual author of the ideas themselves, and that is us. So there is something about ourselves that we can never get at, that we can never define — and in just the same way you cannot bite your own teeth, you cannot hear your own ears, and you cannot make your own hand catch hold of itself. So therefore you must let go and trust the goings-on of your humanness. Confucius was the first to say that he would rather trust human passions and instincts than trust human ideas about what is right, for like the Taoists he realized that we have to allow all living things to look after themselves.

THE WORLD AND ITS OPPOSITES

When we say what things are, we always contrast them with something else, and when we try to talk about the whole universe — about all that there is — we find we really have no words for it. It is "one *what?*"

All of this "one what?" is represented by the symbol of the great circle. But in order to think about life, we have to make comparisons, and so we split it in two and derive from the circle the symbol of the yang and the yin, the positive and the negative.

We see this symbol over and over on Chinese pottery, and today on everything from jewelry to T-shirts. Traditionally this emblem is one of the basic symbols of the philosophy of Taoism. It is the symbol of the yang, or the male, and the yin, the female, of the positive and the negative, the yes and the no, the light and the dark. We always have to divide the world into opposites or categories in order to be able to think about it. In the words of Lao-tzu,

> *When people see some things as beautiful,*
> *other things become ugly.*
> *When people see some things as good,*
> *other things become bad.*
>
> *Being and non-being create each other.*
> *Difficult and easy support each other.*
> *Long and short define each other.*
> *High and low depend on each other.*

Lao-tzu

In the literary tradition of Taoism, the legendary Chinese philosopher Lao-tzu is often referred to as a contemporary of Confucius. According to some accounts, Lao-tzu was supposed to have been a court librarian who wearied of the insincerity and intrigue of court life and decided to leave the city and go off and live in the mountains. But before he left, the guardian of the gate is said to have stopped him and said,

"Sir, I cannot let you go until you write down something of your wisdom."

And it is said that he sat down in the guardhouse and recorded the book known as the *Tao Te Ching*, the book of *Tao* and *Te*, of the Way and its power.

The core of Lao-tzu's written philosophy deals with the art of getting out of one's own way, learning how to act without forcing conclusions, and living in skillful harmony with the processes of nature instead of trying to push them around. Lao-tzu didn't actually say very much about the meaning of Tao; instead, he simply offered his advice.

It is now believed that although this work was probably rendered in a single hand during the time of Confucius, or shortly thereafter, the author incorporated the wisdom of a much older folk tradition. One school believes that Taoist literature was inspired by the oral teaching of shamanic hermits in ancient times. Another holds that the *Tao Te Ching* was an attempt to bring the practical, conventional wisdom of the Chinese people to the ruling class in order to help them to rule with greater wisdom and compassion. Both schools are probably partially correct, and in either case Taoist thought remains among the most accessible of the world's great religious philosophies, and is perhaps the only one to retain a sense of humor.

My favorite picture of Lao-tzu is by the master Sengai, and it shows him in the sort of disheveled and informal style that is so characteristic of Taoist humor, and was later assimilated in Zen Buddhism. This playfulness is one of the most delightful characteristics of the whole of Taoist philosophy and, as a result, I know of no other philosophical works besides those of Lao-tzu and his successor Chuang-tse that are so eminently readable. Of all the great sages of the world, they alone have a sense of the enjoyment of life just as it comes.

Lao-tzu literally means "the old fellow," since Lao means "old" and tzu means "fellow," or sometimes boy. So Lao-tzu is the old boy, and he is sometimes shown as a white-bearded youth, which is of course symbolic of his great wisdom at an early age.*

Long before Buddhism came to China in about 60 A.D., Lao-tzu's philosophy had revealed to the Chinese that you cannot characterize reality, or life itself, as either being or non-being, as either form or emptiness, or by any pair of opposites that you might think of. As he said, "When all the world knows goodness to be good, there is already evil."

We do not know what any of these things are except by contrast with their opposite. For example, it is difficult to see a figure unless there is a contrasting

---

*You will find the writings of both Lao-tzu and his contemporary Chuang-tse in a book called *The Wisdom of Lao-tzu*, translated by Lin Yutang. He has arranged the Lao-tzu book that was supposed to have been written for the guardian of the gate, and then added quite a few substantial excerpts from the book of Chuang-tse as a running commentary on Lao-tzu's passages. [Editor's note: That book is currently out of print. There are of course many other editions in print.]

background. Were there no background to the figure, the figure would vanish, which is the principle of camouflage. Because of the inseparability of opposites, therefore, you realize that they always go together, and this hints at some kind of unity that underlies them.

Tao

In Lao-tzu's philosophy this unity is called *Tao*. Although it is written t-a-o, in Chinese it is pronounced almost as if it were spelled d-o-w. It has the sense of a rhythmic motion, of going on and stopping, and also a sense of intelligence, and so you get an idea of a sort of rhythmic intelligence that ebbs and flows like the tides.

The word has two general meanings. One is perhaps

best rendered into English as "the way," "the way of things," or "the way of nature." The other sense of the word means "to speak," so when the opening words of Lao-tzu's book say,

The Tao that can be spoken is not the eternal Tao,

it makes a pun in Chinese. It says literally, "The Tao that can be Tao is not Tao," or if you read it like a telegram, "Tao can Tao no Tao." The first meaning of Tao is "the way," and the second meaning of it is "to speak," or in other words,

The way that can be expressed is not the eternal way.

I prefer not to translate the word Tao at all because to us Tao is a sort of nonsense syllable, indicating the mystery that we can never understand — the unity that underlies the opposites. In our deepest intuition we know that there is some sort of unity underlying these various opposites because we find that we can't separate one from the other. We know that a whole universe exists, but we can't really say what it is. So

Tao is thus a reality that we apprehend deeply without being able to define it.

A Chinese poet put it this way:

> *Plucking chrysanthemums along the eastern fence,*
> *gazing in silence at the southern hills,*
> *the birds fly home in pairs,*
> *through the soft mountain air of dusk.*
> *In all these things there is a deep meaning,*
> *but when we're about to express it,*
> *we suddenly forget the words.*

Lao-tzu also said, "Those who speak, do not know; those who know, do not speak." And another Chinese poet satirized him by saying, "Those who speak, do not know; those who know, do not speak; thus we have heard from Lao-tzu, and yet how does it come that he himself wrote a book of five hundred characters?" The point, then, is that his whole book does not in any way define what the Tao means. He speaks not so much about it, but rather speaks with it, using it, as it were, as the power by which to express himself.

So what is the reason why Tao is inexpressible and yet at the same time the basis for a philosophy? The reason is that we cannot have any system of thought — whether it be philosophical, or logical, or mathematical, or physical — which defines its own basis. This is an extremely important principle to understand. In other words, I can pick up a paint brush with my right hand, but I can't pick up my right hand. My right hand picks itself up. If I try to pick up my hand, what would I pick it up with? There always has to be something, as it were, that isn't picked up, that picks itself up, that works itself and is not worked upon.

In the same way, you will find that if you look up "to be" in a dictionary, it is defined as "to exist." Then when you look up "to exist," you will find it defined as "to be." And are you any the wiser? A dictionary cannot really completely define itself; ultimately it can only put words together that correspond to other words.

In this sense, to try to say anything about the Tao is like trying to eat your own mouth, and of course you cannot get outside of it to eat it. Or to put it the other way, anything you can chew is not your mouth. Anything that is expressed about the Tao is not the Tao.

Tzu-Jan
By Itself So

There is always something that we don't know. This is well illustrated by the elusive qualities of energy in physics: We cannot really define energy, but we can work with it, and this is the case with the Tao. The Tao works by itself. Its nature is to be, as is said in Chinese, *tzu-jan*, that which is "of itself," "by itself," or "itself so." Tzu-jan is almost what we mean when we say that something is automatic, or that something happens automatically. We sometimes translate this expression in English as "nature," as when we talk about the nature of the mountains, the birds, the bees, and the flowers. That sort of nature in Chinese would be tzu-jan.

The fundamental sense of it is that the Tao operates of itself. All that is natural operates of itself, and there is nothing standing over it and making it go on. In the same way one's own body operates of itself. You don't have to decide when and how you're going to beat your heart; it just happens. You don't decide exactly how you are going to breathe; your lungs fill and empty themselves without effort. You don't determine the structure of your own nervous system or of your bones; they grow all by themselves.

So the Tao goes along of itself. And since there is always a basic element of life that cannot be defined — in the same way the Tao cannot be defined — it cannot be controlled. In other words, you can't get outside yourself to define yourself or to control yourself. Lao-tzu would go on to say that since man is an integral part of the natural universe, he cannot hope to control it as if it were an object quite separate from himself. You can't get outside of nature to be the master of nature. Remember that your heart beats "self-so" — and, if you give it a chance, your mind can function "self-so," although most of us are afraid to give it a chance.

Wu Wei

Not Forcing

Whenever we have the feeling of being able to dominate ourselves, master ourselves, or become the lords of nature, what happens is that we do not really succeed in getting outside of nature or of ourselves at all. Instead we have forced our way of seeing these things to conform to an illusion that makes us think they are controlled objects, and in doing this we invariably set up a conflict inside the system. We soon find that the tension between our idea of things and things as they are puts us out of accord with the way of things.

For this reason you might say that *not-forcing* is the second principle of the Tao — the spontaneous or *of-itself-so* activity (tzu-jan) being the first. In Chinese the second principle is called *wu wei*, and it means literally "not doing," but would be much better translated to give it the spirit of "not forcing" or "not obstructing." In reference to the Tao it is the sense that the activity of nature is not self-obstructive. It all works together as a unity and does not, as it were, split apart from itself to do something to itself.

Wu wei is also applied to human activity, and refers to a person who does not get in his or her own way. One does not stand in one's own light while working, and so the way of wu wei (this sounds like a pun but it isn't) is the way of non-obstruction or non-interference. This is the preeminently practical Taoist principle of life.

What I mean by forcing yourself is something like this: When children in school are supposed to be paying attention to the teacher, their thoughts will go wandering all over the place, and the teacher will soon get angry and say, "Pay attention." And the children will wrap their legs around the legs of the chair, and they will stare at the teacher and try to look frightfully intelligent. But what happens was expressed very well in a cartoon I saw the other day: A small boy is standing and looking at his teacher and saying, "I'm sorry, I didn't hear what you were saying because I was listening so hard." In other words, when we try to be loving, or to be virtuous, or to be sincere, we actually think about trying to do it in the same way the child was trying to listen, tightening up his muscles and trying to look intelligent as he thought about paying attention. But he wasn't thinking about what the teacher is saying, and therefore he wasn't really listening at all. This is a perfect example of what is meant by blocking yourself or getting in your own light.

To offer another illustration of it, suppose you are cutting wood. If you go against the way the tree grew, that is to say against the grain of the wood, the wood is very difficult to cut. If you go with the grain, however, it splits easily. Or again, in sawing wood, some people are in a great hurry to get on with sawing and they try and power right through the piece. But what happens? When you turn the board over you see the back edge of the wood is full of splinters, and you find that you are rather tired as well. Any skilled carpenter will tell you, "Let the saw do the work, let the teeth do the cutting." And you find that by going at it quite easily, and just allowing the blade to glide back and forth, the wood is easily cut.

As our own proverb says, "Easy does it." And wu wei means easy does it. Look out for the grain of things, the way of things. Move in accord with it and work is thereby made simple.

Te

Virtue: Skill at Living

In one book the philosopher Chuang-tse tells a wonderful story about a butcher who was able to keep the same chopper for twenty years because he was always careful to let the blade fall on the interstices between the bones. And so in this way he never wore it out.

Once again we see that the person who learns the kind of activity which is, shall we say, in accord with the Tao, is said to possess virtue. This peculiar Chinese sense of virtue is called *Te*, but it is not virtue in quite our ordinary sense of being good. Te is like our word virtue when it is used more in the sense of the healing virtues of a plant. When we use the word virtue in this way it really designates an extraordinary kind of skill at living. And in his book Lao-tzu says the superior kind of virtue is not conscious of itself as virtue, and thus really is virtue. But the inferior kind of virtue is so anxious to be virtuous that it loses its virtue altogether.

We often come upon the kind of virtuous person who is self-consciously virtuous, who has, you might say, too much virtue. These are the sorts of people who are a perpetual challenge to all their friends, and when you are in their presence you feel they are so good that you don't know quite what to say. And so you are always, as it were, sitting on the edge of your chair and feeling a little bit uncomfortable in their presence. In a Taoist way of speaking, this kind of person stinks of virtue, and doesn't really have any virtue at all.

The truly virtuous person is unobtrusive. It is not that they are affectedly modest; instead they are what they are quite naturally. Lao-tzu says that the greatest intelligence appears to be stupidity, the greatest eloquence sounds like a stammer, and the greatest brightness appears as if it were dull. And of course this is a kind of paradoxical way of saying that true virtue, Te, is the living of human life in such a fashion as not to get in its own way.

This is the thing we all admire and envy so much about children. We say that they are naive, that they are unspoiled, that they are artless, and that they are unself-conscious. When you see a little child dancing who has not yet learned to dance before an audience, you can see the child dancing all by itself, and there is a kind of completeness and genuine integrity to their motion.

When the child then sees that parents or teachers are watching, and learns that they may approve or disapprove, the child begins to watch itself while dancing. All at once the dancing becomes stiff, and then becomes artful, or worse, artificial, and the spirit of the child's dance is lost. But if the child happens to go on studying dance, it is only after years and years that, as an accomplished artist, the dancer regains the naivete and the naturalness of their original dance. But when the naturalness is regained it is not just the simple, we could say embryonic, naturalness of the child, completely uncultivated and untutored. Instead it is a new kind of naturalness that takes into itself and carries with itself years and years of technique, know-how, and experience.

In all this you will see that there are three stages. There is first what we might call the natural or the childlike stage of life in which self-consciousness has not yet arisen. Then there comes a middle stage, which we might call one's awkward age, in which one learns to become self-conscious. And finally the two are integrated in the rediscovered innocence of a liberated person.

Of course there is a tremendous advantage in this, because one must ask, if you are enjoying life without knowing that you are enjoying it, are you really enjoying it? And here, of course, consciousness offers an enormous advantage. But there is also a disadvantage, even a danger, in developing it, because as consciousness grows, and as we begin to know how to look at ourselves and beyond ourselves, we may start over and over again, and cause much interference with our-selves. This is when we begin to get in our own light.

You know how it is when you get in your own light or get in your own way — when it becomes desper-ately essential that you hurry to catch a train or plane, for example, instead of your muscles being relaxed and ready to run, your anxiety about not getting there in time immediately stiffens you up and you start stum-bling over everything. It is the same sort of thing on those days when everything goes absolutely wrong. First of all, when you're driving to the office, all the traffic lights are against you. Of course this irritates you, and because of your irritation you become more tense and more uptight in your way of handling things, and this leads to mistakes. It could lead to being so furious and going so fast that the police stop you, and so on and so forth. It is this way of battering against life, as it were, that ties it up in knots.

And so, the secret in Taoism is to get out of one's own way, and to learn that this pushing ourselves, instead of making us more efficient, actually interferes with everything we set about to do.

PART II

THE GENTLE WAY

The Tao is like a well:
used but never used up.
It is like the eternal void:
filled with infinite possibilities....

The Tao is called the Great Mother,
empty yet inexhaustible,
it gives birth to infinite worlds.

It is always present within you.
You can use it any way you want.

The Strength of Weakness

Lao-tzu writes about the philosophy of the strength of weakness. It is a strange thing, I think, how it is men in the West do not realize how much softness is strength. One of old Lao-tzu's favorite analogies was water. He spoke of water as the weakest of all things in the world, and yet there is nothing to be compared with it in overcoming what is hard and strong. You can cut water with a knife and it lets the knife go right through, yet water alone cut the Grand Canyon out of solid rock.

Lao-tzu also said that while being a man, one should retain a certain essential feminine element, and that he who does this will become a channel for the whole world.

The ideal of the hundred-percent tough guy, the rigid, rugged fellow with muscles like steel, is really a model for weakness. We probably assume this sort of tough exterior will work as a hard shell to protect ourselves — but so much of what we fear from the outside gets to us because we fear our own weakness on the inside.

What happens if an engineer builds a completely rigid bridge? If, for example, the Golden Gate Bridge or George Washington Bridge did not sway in the wind, and if they had no give, and no yielding, they would come crashing down. And so you can always be sure that when a man pretends to be 100 percent male on the outside, he is in doubt of his manhood somewhere on the inside. If he can allow himself to be weak, he can allow himself to experience what is really his greatest strength. This is so not only of human beings, but of all living things.

JUDO
The Gentle Way

The philosophy of the strength of weakness that came from China to Japan through the migration of Zen Buddhism has inspired the astonishing forms of self-defense known as judo and akido. The word *judo* is fascinating because it means *ju*, the gentle, *do*, way. *Do* is the Japanese way of pronouncing the Chinese Tao, and so it is the gentle Tao, the philosophy of the Tao as applied to self-defense.

This philosophy has various components, and one of the most basic elements to the whole practice of judo is an understanding of balance — and balance, indeed, is a fundamental idea in Taoist philosophy. The philosophy of the Tao has a basic respect for the balance of nature, and if you are sensitive you don't upset that balance. Instead you try to find out what it is doing, and go along with it.

In other words you avoid such mistakes as the wholesale slaughter of an insect pest or the introduction of rabbits into a country like Australia without thought as to whether they have a natural enemy, because through such interference with the balance of nature you inevitably find yourself in trouble. The philosophy of balance is the first thing that all students of judo and akido have to learn, and it is the underlying principle of the Tao.

If we look at the principles of judo, the question of balance is easily demonstrated by looking at what happens when we try to lift a heavy roll of material. We would be foolish to try and just pick it up from the top, because that shows no understanding of the laws of balance. If you want to lift something, go below its center of gravity. Put your shoulder to it, undermine it, and then swoop it up. That principle follows throughout judo. Part of the understanding of balance in judo is to learn to walk in such a way that you are never off center: your legs form the base of a triangle, and your body is on the apex, and when you turn you always try to keep your feet approximately under your shoulders, and in this way you are never off balance. This is a good practice in everyday life as well as in judo.

The second principle, beyond understanding and keeping balance, is not to oppose strength with strength. When you are attacked by the enemy, you do not oppose him. Instead you yield to him, just like the matador yields to the bull, and you use his strength and the principle of balance to bring about his downfall.

Suppose, for example, there is a blow coming at me from a certain direction. Instead of defending myself, and pushing the blow off, the idea in judo is to carry the blow away. But as the adversary goes by, the knee goes out, catching him below his point of balance. The adversary then falls heavy and hard — brought about by his own initiative, and your receptivity. By letting him follow his punch through, and not deflecting it, he has fallen into your trap.

The same attitude of relaxed gentleness is most beautifully seen when you watch cats climbing trees. When a cat falls out of a tree, it lets go of itself. The cat becomes completely relaxed, and lands lightly on the ground. But if a cat were about to fall out of a tree and suddenly made up its mind that it didn't want to fall, it would become tense and rigid, and would be just a bag of broken bones upon landing.

In the same way, it is the philosophy of the Tao that we are all falling off a tree, at every moment of our lives. As a matter of fact, the moment we were born we were kicked off a precipice and we are falling, and there is nothing that can stop it. So instead of living in a state of chronic tension, and clinging to all sorts of things that are actually falling with us because the whole world is impermanent, be like a cat. Don't resist it.

LI

The Patterns of Nature

Thus far, like a typical philosopher, I have been trying to explain what Taoism is, and odd as it may seem, this is really quite the wrong thing to do.

Stranger still, if I succeed in giving you some sort of impression that you really understand, if I succeed in making the whole problem clear in words, I shall have deceived you. One reason life seems problematic to us, and one reason why we look to philosophy to try to clear it all up, is that we have been trying to fit the order of the universe to the order of words. And it simply does not work.

Yet I continue to talk and write about Eastern philosophy, and I have often said that the real basis of Buddhism is not a set of ideas but an experience. This of course is equally true of Taoism as well, which like Buddhism recognizes that experience is altogether something different from words. If you have tasted a certain taste, even the taste of water, you know what it is. But to someone who has not tasted it, it can never be explained in words because it goes far beyond words.

The order of the world is very different from the order we create with the rules of our syntax and grammar. The order of the world is extraordinarily complex, while the order of words is relatively simple, and to use the order of words to try to explain life is really as clumsy an operation as trying to drink water with a fork. Our confusion of the order of logic and of words with the order of nature is what makes everything seem so problematic to us.

When we say that we are trying to make sense out of life, that means that we are trying to treat the real world as if it were a collection of words. Words are symbols, and they mean something other than signs formed out of letters, but actual people, mountains, rivers, and stars are neither symbols nor signs. And so the difficulty that we encounter in trying to make sense out of life is that we are trying to fit the very complex order of life itself into a very simple system that is not up to the task, and this gets us involved in all sorts of unforeseen difficulties.

In the Chinese language there are two terms that signify these two different orders. The first is the word *tsu*, which means "the order of things as measured," or "the order of things as written down." In one sense this word has the meaning of "law," and although we sometimes speak of the laws of nature, the laws of nature could never be *tsu* unless we made an attempt to describe them or write them down in order to think about them in words.

Since *tsu* only refers to the order of things as we think about them in words or numbers, the Chinese use another word, *li*, for the actual order of nature. This is a peculiar and interesting term; its original meaning is the markings in jade, the grain in wood, or the fiber in muscle, and it has been translated by the great student of Chinese thought, Joseph Needham, as "organic pattern." It refers to the kind of complex pattern we see when we look at the stars, for example, and see a gaseous nebula, which is an extremely indeterminate form, or when we look at the sculpted layers forming the patterns in a rock, and see the glorious rippling that is incredibly difficult to describe, although easy enough to understand with our eyes and our feelings. But to try to put that kind of order into words is always beyond us, and it is for this reason that the attempt to make sense out of life will always fail.

The order of *li*, of the infinite complexity of organic pattern, is also the order of our own bodies, and of our brains and nervous systems. We actually live by that order, for as I have often noted we do not figure out in words or ordered thoughts how we grow our own bodies, structure our bones, or regulate our metabolism. In fact we really have no idea how we manage to do any of this, no idea how we manage to be conscious, how we actually think, and how we actually make decisions. We do these things, but the processes and the order of the physical body that underlies them are completely mysterious to us. Even though we can do these things, we cannot fully describe them.

All the time we are actually relying on this strange and unintelligible form of natural order. It is at the basis of everything we do, and even when we try to figure something out and describe it in words, and then make a decision on the basis of that process, we are still unconsciously relying upon an order that we cannot figure out. That order constitutes our basic nature, but we are too close to it to see it — and so following the Tao is the art of feeling our way into our own nature.

In the process of our upbringing, however, and particularly in our education, our parents and teachers are very careful to teach us not to rely on our spontaneous abilities. We are taught to figure things out, and our first task is to learn the different names for everything. In this way we learn to treat all of the things of the world as separate objects.

A tree is a tree, and it begins with its roots, and ends with the leaves on its branches, and that's that. We are also taught to behave consistently, almost as if we are characters in a book, and you know how the critics hate an author who doesn't make his characters consistent. If we were actually consistent in life it would be very boring, but I think that sometimes, in this respect, we take our cues for living from literature, and attempt to impose a consistency on top of our natural, ever-changing spontaneity.

Since we are brought up to make sense of ourselves, and to be able to account for ourselves, we are always expected to be able to rationalize our actions in words. When we try to accomplish this we develop a kind of second self inside us, which in Zen is called the observing self. This observing self can be a very good thing for us to develop, and it can also cause problems, and run a commentary on who we are and what we are doing all the time. It asks, "What will other people say? Am I being proper? Does what I am doing make any sense?"

The sociologist George Herbert Meade called this "the interiorized other." That is to say, we have a kind of interior picture, a vague sense of who we are, and of what the reaction of other people to us says about who we are. That reaction is almost invariably communicated to us through what other people say and think, but soon we learn to maintain the commentary on our own, and each thought or observation is then compared to the idea we have formed. Therefore this image becomes interiorized — a second self who is commenting all the time upon what the first one is doing — and in any given situation we must either rationalize why a certain behavior is consistent with that image, or force ourselves to change that behavior, or fail to change it and feel guilty for failing. The difficulty with this is that although it is exceedingly important for all purposes of civilized intercourse and personal relationships to be able to make sense of what we are doing, and of what other people are doing, and to be able to talk about it all in words, this nevertheless warps us.

We have all admired the spontaneity and freshness of children, and it is regrettable that as children are brought up they become more and more self-conscious. In this way people often lose their freshness, and more and more human beings seem to be turned into creatures calculated to get in their own way.

Humans get in their own way because they are always observing and questioning themselves. They are always trying to fit the order of the world into the order of sense, the order of thought and words. And therefore the children lose their naturalness and spontaneity. For this reason we admire the people, whether they be sages or artists, who have the ability to return in their mature life to a kind of childlikeness and freshness. They are not bothered any more by what people are thinking or saying. This is the charm that surrounds the Taoist sages of ancient China.

I Ching
Book of Changes

For an illustration of the pattern intelligence of *li*, and of how it can be used in decision making, let's look at an ancient Chinese method of divination that is infused and linked inextricably with Taoism. Perhaps you know of divination as a kind of fortune-telling, but this particular form of divination is based on what some people believe to be the very oldest of all the Chinese tracts, the *I Ching*, or the *Book of Changes*. As such, I think one would not presume to ask such an ancient and honored book of wisdom as the *I Ching* what to bet on the stock market, but rather one asks questions about one's spiritual or psychological state or consults the oracle concerning momentous decisions in life.

The old and orthodox way of consulting the *Book of Changes* is to use the stalks of a yarrow plant, which are long, straight, and narrow. A number of stalks are taken and divided at random, and then the calculations are made. But this is a rather long and elaborate way of casting, and the not-so-ancient but equally respectable way is to use coins. I keep three Chinese coins for this purpose; any other coins work just as well.

The kind of question to ask the *Book of Changes* that would be appropriate under most circumstances is something like this: "What is the best thing for me in my present state?" We phrase a clear question, and then take the coins and shake them and drop them; according to the way they fall on each toss — heads or tails — we construct a six-line hexagram consisting of a pair of three-line trigrams.

It works like this: We shake and throw all three

coins together at the same time; each throw of the three coins gives us a single line. The inscribed side of the Chinese coin —or the "tails" side of an American coin — counts as yin, with the value of 2. The reverse side — or the "heads" side of an American coin — counts as yang, with a value of 3. There are then four different possibilities for the three coins:

If all the coins are yin, the total value of all three coins is 6, and a broken line, or negative line, is drawn, and forms the bottom line of the hexagram. This is the so-called "old yin" line:

If two coins are yin and one is yang, the total value is 7, and an unbroken, or positive, line is drawn, the so-called "young yang" line:

If one coin is yin and two are yang, the total value is 8, and a broken, or negative, line, the so-called "young yin," is drawn. And if all three coins are yang, the total value is 9, and an unbroken, or positive, line is drawn: the "old yang."

Let's look at a particular case, and assume that on the first throw we get a total of 6, a negative reading, and the symbol that records the negative reading is the drawing of a broken line, a yin line.

We do it again, and this time the total is 8 — the reading is again negative, and again we record it, and draw another broken line on top of the first broken line, beginning to create our hexagram from the bottom to the top.

We shake them again, drop the coins, and this time the total is 7 — a positive reading. We record this toss by an unbroken line, or a yang line representing the positive principle, and the first trigram is completed.

We throw again, and once more the total is 6 and the line is negative. And again, and the total is

8 and the line is once more negative. And then we throw a final, sixth time, and the total is 9, and the line is indisputable: an unbroken, yang line goes on the top.

And so we arrive at this figure:

In order to know what it means we have to take a look at a very ancient diagram, one that may be familiar to you. Perhaps you've seen it on Chinese bowls or jewelry or carving in jade. These are the eight *trigrams* — symbols composed of three vertically stacked lines — arranged in a circle, and in the center of the design, you see the figure we saw earlier, the symbol of the yang and the yin principles.[*]

In China the symbol in the center is also known

_____

[*]You will find the picture at the beginning of this section (page 66).

as *Tai Chi*, the symbol for the two fundamental principles, the positive and the negative, the yang and the yin that are held to lie at the root of all phenomena in the world. The Chinese character for the word yang looks like a fish; it represents the light side, and means the southern or bright side of a mountain. The character for yin is the black fish; it represents the shady or dark side of a mountain. Respectively, as we have seen, they represent the male and the female principles.

Notice the symbolism of a light and dark side of a mountain — you do not find a mountain with only one side; the two sides must always go together. And so, in the same way, the Chinese feel that the positive and the negative, the light and the dark, the male and the female, the auspicious and the inauspicious always go together in human life, because one cannot be distinguished without the other.

Outside the rotating figure of the positive and negative principles you will find the eight trigrams, which are every possible combination of broken or unbroken lines. These trigrams represent the eight fundamental principles or elements that, according to the *Book of Changes*, are involved in every life situation.

The one at the top, for example, means heaven, or sky, which is symbolic of the creative principle, and the one directly below means earth, and is symbolic of the receptive principle. In the Chinese system each trigram also corresponds to a family member, and the creative symbol is the father, the receptive symbol the mother.

Over on one side, we find a trigram with two yang or radiant lines enclosing a receptive line, and it is associated with the element of fire and means clinging, or perhaps holding. Opposite, the trigram has two receptive lines surrounding a receptive line, and is associated with water, and with the chasm and the dangerous abyss. Between the four cardinal trigrams appear the four intercardinal trigrams: thunder, wind, lake, and mountain. Within the oracle, every situation in life may be represented by two of these principles in preponderance. In our example above, one trigram is repeated twice, and what we have cast is a mountain over a mountain.

ADVICE FROM THE ORACLE

Altogether there are sixty-four possible combinations of these eight trigrams, which makes the meaning of each combination pretty difficult to remember. So now we will look to the *Book of Changes* itself to see what it has to say about this particular hexagram, and what advice the oracle would want to give us in answer to our question about our present situation.

The mountain over the mountain happens to be number 52, called, not surprisingly, "the Mountain." The figure of the mountain is a symbol associated with the idea of quietness, or keeping still. And when we have "keeping still" or "quietness" above "quietness," we have before us a whole emblem whose meaning is profound calm.

And so the oracle says,

THE JUDGMENT

Keeping still. Keeping his back still
So that he no longer feels his body.

He goes into his courtyard
And does not see his people.
No blame.

True quiet means keeping still when
the time has come to keep still, and going
forward when the time has come to go forward. In this way rest and movement are in
agreement with the demands of the time,
and thus there is light in life....

THE IMAGE

Mountains standing close together:
The image of 耆keeping still.
Thus the superior man
Does not permit his thoughts
To go beyond his situation.

The heart thinks constantly. This cannot
be changed. But the movements of the heart
— that is, a man's thoughts — should restrict
themselves to the immediate situation. All

thinking that goes beyond this only makes the heart sore.*

You can see that this is pretty generalized advice, and it is in a way appropriate to the question because the question was vague, and so the answer is vague. But the symbolism of this answer is simply that sitting so as to keep one's back still, so that one's back is not noticed, is self-forgetfulness. And keeping one's thoughts to the immediate situation suggests the practice of meditation or calmness or quietness. That's what we're advised to do. It's good advice.

A WESTERN POINT OF VIEW

You may well say, however, that this is a thoroughly crazy way of coming to decisions, especially if I were to ask something more specific than this, or

---

*Reprinted by permission of the Princeton University Press from *The I Ching or Book of Changes*, the Richard Wilhelm translation, © 1950 by Bollingen Foundation, Inc.

if I had asked advice on some momentous decision I had to make. We would say, from our modern, scientific point of view, that flipping coins to come to the great decisions of life is the stupidest thing one could possibly do. After all, it neglects all rational cogitation about our situations. It takes no account of the data available in the situation. It makes no intelligent assessment of the probabilities, and before we make any important decision, we like to think over all the factors involved.

We go into the situation and think it out thoroughly. We balance the pros against the cons, and we balance assets against deficits. And therefore we believe that nothing could be more superstitious than relying upon an oracle that in turn relies entirely on the random chance of falling coins. We know that the coins have no relation to the problem whatsoever, and so naturally our contemporary point of view about this — and all other methods of fortune-telling, divination, and so on — is that if they work at all, it is nothing more than pure chance.

AN EASTERN POINT OF VIEW

To someone who believes in this system, however, perhaps a traditional Chinese or Japanese person, it does not seem farfetched at all. They might say to us, "First of all, when you consider the facts that are involved in any particular decision, and calculate all the data, how do you select which facts are most relevant?

"If you are going to enter into a business contract, for instance, perhaps the facts you believe pertain to this contract are the state of your own business, the state of the other person's business, and the prospects of the market, but you probably would not think about many of the personal matters that might affect the plan. And nevertheless, something that you may never have considered at all may enter into the situation and change it completely. The person you're going into business with may slip on a banana peel and get seriously injured and become inefficient or even detrimental in the business. How could anyone ever predict such an eventuality by taking a sane and rational assessment of the situation?"

Or perhaps they might say to us, "How do you know when you have collected enough data? After all, the data and the potential problems involved in any particular situation are virtually infinite. What causes you to stop collecting data, or stop gathering information about how to solve a problem? I think you just collect information until you are either tired of collecting it, or until the time comes to act and you have run out of time to collect more data." And one could present a very convincing argument that because you decide when to stop investigating in a very arbitrary way, this method is just as arbitrary as flipping coins.

PROBABILITIES AND DECISIONS

"Well," we could argue, "what about probabilities? After all, we rely a great deal upon statistics in order to make decisions." But statistics have their limitations — they work very well when averaging what a large number of people are going to do, but are useless in individual cases. The actuarial tables used by insurance companies, for example, will tell you quite accurately the average life span of an adult male or female, smoker or nonsmoker, but in any individual case these tables will not tell us when someone is going to die. And the same is probably true if we look at any given decision that we may make: The probability is that we will weigh all the information, and in the final moment make our decision based upon our "hunch," which is really a gut feeling about the situation that has little to do with rational thought.

Now I am of a somewhat skeptical temperament, and I very much doubt if in fact this way of coming to decisions really works. But I say this with a certain qualification, because we can never really prove whether any method of coming to a decision really works. I may make a supremely foolish decision and as a result of it I get killed, but there would be absolutely no way of showing that my getting killed at that moment did not preserve me from a worse fate, and perhaps from making mistakes that involve the lives of many other people. If I do happen to succeed by making a right decision in business affairs and I earn millions of dollars, there is likewise no way of showing that this was not so bad for my character that it was the worst thing that could have possibly happened. So we never really know whether the outcome of a decision will be a failure or a success in the long run, because only the unknown — only what comes next — will show whether it was good or bad. And the unknown stretches infinitely before us.

DISADVANTAGES AND ADVANTAGES

There are advantages and disadvantages to both modern scientific inquiry and to the system of this old Chinese book of divination. There is a bad side to the *Book of Changes* and a distinct disadvantage in Chinese culture. The Chinese came to rely so much on the *Book of Changes* and its system of symbols for classifying all natural phenomena that in the course of time it became a very rigid structure and eventually excluded the perception of novelty.

The warning for us in this, whereby we might

take advantage of their mistake, is to realize that we are doing the same thing with scientific method. There are certain kinds of personalities who tend to become very rigid in their scientific ideas and thereafter automatically exclude certain possibilities because they do not happen to conform with alleged scientific dogma.

Take for example what we call ESP, or extrasensory perception, although I prefer to call it extraordinary sensory perception. There is extremely strong evidence that perception of this kind occurs, and yet many scientific people will ignore that evidence because they say that it simply can't happen. Limiting their inquiry in this way is to fall into the same rut that the Chinese fell into when they relied too exclusively upon the classification of the world and of events found in the *Book of Changes*.

Both systems, on the other hand, have their advantages. Just as there is a positive use for science, there is a positive side to the *Book of Changes*. The picture seen in the book through the interplay of these forms is founded on a view of life that is very suggestive to us of a new way of looking at our information, and is in accord with certain points of view that are now developing in our own science. It is a way of looking at life that focuses on not so much the causal relationship between the events, as the pattern of events as a whole.

A COMPARISON OF EAST AND WEST

Let me try to show the difference between these two ways of investigation. When we think of causality, we think chiefly of the way events are determined by the past, and by extension the way the behavior of people is determined by their past. It is as if events were a lot of different marbles that are thrown together and knock each other around. In tracing the movement of any particular marble, therefore, we will try to find out which other marbles knocked it about, and so trace its individual history further and further back. Until quite recent times the point of view of Western science was based almost exclusively on the idea of causality; it had become a study of the way things are influenced by past things.

The point of view that underlies the *Book of Changes* is that instead of trying to understand events as relationships to past causes, it understands events by relation to their present pattern. In other words, it comprehends them by taking a total view of the organism and its environment instead of what we might call a linear view. Although the Chinese have not really applied this approach to their technology, they have traditionally applied it to their art and to their philosophy of natural law, and their essential point of view is quite different from ours.

We can find a suitable analogy for the Western way of looking at things by saying that we are attempting to understand events in accordance with the order of words. I can say, "This dog has no bark," and then say, "This tree has no bark," and the meaning of "bark" in these two sentences is determined by what went before them — so if I want to know what "bark" means, I have to go back to what happened in the past.

If you look at what I would rather call the order of design, however, and not the order of words, you find a rather different situation because all of the elements of the design come at you together. They are, as we would say, "of a piece," and you see their relationship to their context and meaning all at once, much as you see the image appear when you develop a photographic plate. The meaning of each part of the design is relative to the rest of the design just as you see it at this moment.

In the same way, the fundamental philosophy of the *Book of Changes* and of the Chinese idea of the relationship between events is to understand every event in its present context. We do not understand something by what went before so much as we do by understanding it in terms of what goes with it. So the idea of the *Book of Changes* is to review through its symbols the total pattern of the moment when the question is asked, and the supposition is that the pattern of this moment governs even the tossing of the coins.

The interesting comparison that arises out of this comes about because we in the West have tended to understand events in accordance with linear or sequential orders like the order of words.

In accordance with the rules of causality, we have evolved or constructed a conception of nature based on the structure of written law.

But in the Chinese language we come again to *li*, the word for natural law that originally meant the markings in jade, the grain in wood, or the fiber in muscle, which is really the basic fundamental pattern of things. Images such as the markings in jade or the grain in wood are used because they have an extremely subtle, complex pattern that shows a large area of events all happening together at once. These patterns have to be taken in and understood at a glance, in the same way as we take in a design at a glance.

The fundamental Chinese idea of the order of nature is not compatible with formulation in the order of words, because it is organic, and is not linear pattern.

In other words, when we think of beauty we know very clearly what beauty is, but it is absolutely impossible to write down a set of laws and rules that can show us how to create beautiful objects. And mathematicians, for example, often feel that certain equations, certain expressions are peculiarly beautiful. Because they are meticulous people, they try to think out exactly why they are beautiful, and ask if we could make up a rule or formula to describe when beauty will or will not appear. Although they have proposed the criteria of elegance as a new kind of proof to be considered, their general conclusion is that if we could make up a rule and apply it in mathematics, and if we could always by the use of this rule get a beautiful result, eventually those results would cease to impress us as being beautiful. They would become sterile and dry.

And in the same way, the order of nature, the order of justice, and the order of beauty are things that we can know in ourselves, yet we cannot write down in black and white. The wiser person, therefore, is one who has the sensibility to see those things in themselves, and to know that beauty lies in the variability of experience from one situation to another.

Conclusion

Ultimately, of course, it is absolutely impossible to understand and appreciate our natural universe unless you know when to stop investigating.

In our restlessness we are always tempted to climb every hill and cross every skyline to find out what lies beyond, yet as you get older and wiser it is not just flagging energy but wisdom that teaches you to look at mountains from below, or perhaps just climb them a little way. For at the top you can no longer see the mountain. And beyond, on the other side, there is, perhaps, just another valley like this.

An old aphorism from India says, "What is

beyond, is that which is also here."

And you must not mistake this for a kind of blasé boredom, or a tiring of adventure. It is instead the startling recognition that in the place where we are now, we have already arrived.

This is it.

What we are seeking is, if we are not totally blind, already here.

For if you must follow that trail up the mountainside to its bitter end, you will discover that it leads eventually right back into the suburbs. But only an exceedingly stupid person will think that is where the trail really goes. For the actual truth is the trail goes to every single place that it crosses, and leads also to where you are standing and watching it. Watching it vanish into the hills, you are already in the truth beyond, which it leads to ultimately.

Many a time I have had intense delight listening to some hidden waterfall in the mountain canyon, a sound made all the more wonderful since I have set aside the urge to ferret the thing out, and clear up the mystery. I no longer need to find out just where the stream comes from and where it goes. Every stream, every road, if followed persistently and meticulously to its end, leads nowhere at all.

And this is why the compulsively investigative mind is always ending up in what it believes to be the hard and bitter reality of the actual facts. Playing a violin is, after all, only scraping a cat's entrails with horsehair. The stars in heaven are, after all, only radioactive rocks and gas. But this is nothing more than the delusion that truth is to be found only by picking everything to pieces like a spoiled child picking at its food.

And this is also why the Platos of the Far East so seldom tell all, and why they avoid filling in every detail. This is why they leave in their paintings great areas of emptiness and vagueness, and yet the paintings are not unfinished. These are not just unfilled backgrounds, they are integral parts of the whole composition, suggestive and pregnant voids and rifts that leave something to our imagination. And we do not make the mistake of trying to fill them in with detail in the mind's eye. We let them remain suggestive.

So it is not by pushing relentlessly and aggressively beyond those hills that we discover the unknown and persuade nature to disclose her secrets. What is beyond is also here.

Any place where we are may be considered the center of the universe. Anywhere that we stand can be considered the destination of our journey.

To understand this, however, we have to be receptive and open. In other words, we have to do what Lao-tzu advised when he said that while being a man one should also preserve a certain femininity, and thereby one will become a channel for the whole universe. And this is not just good advice for men.

Yet that is one of the misunderstandings in which I believe our culture in the West is submerged. The feminine values are despised, and we find typically among men a strange kind of reluctance to be anything but an all-male man.

But there is a tremendous necessity for us to value — alongside, as it were, the aggressive, masculine element symbolized by the sword — the receptive feminine element symbolized, perhaps, by the open flower. After all, our human senses are not knives, they are not hooks; they are the soft veil of the eye, the delicate drum of the ear, the soft skin on the tips of the fingers and on the body. It is through these delicate, receptive things that we receive our knowledge of the world.

And therefore it is only through a kind of weakness and softness that it is possible for knowledge to come to us.

To put it another way, we have to come to terms with nature by wooing her rather than fighting her, and instead of holding nature at a distance through our objectivity as if she were an enemy, realize rather that she is to be known by her embrace.

In the end, we must decide what we really want to know about.

Do we trust nature, or would we rather try to manage the whole thing?

Do we want to be some kind of omnipotent god, in control of it all, or do we want to enjoy it instead? After all, we can't enjoy what we are anxiously trying to control. One of the nicest things about our bodies is that we don't have to think about them all the time. If when you woke up in the morning you had to think about every detail of your circulation, you would never get through the day.

It was well said: "The mystery of life is not a problem to be solved, but a reality to be experienced."

The song of birds, the voices of insects are all means of conveying truth to the mind. In flowers and grasses we see messages of the Tao.

The scholar, pure and clear of mind, serene and open of heart, should find in everything what nourishes him.

But if you want to know where the flowers come from, even the god of spring doesn't know.

About the Author

Alan Watts was born in England in 1915. Beginning at age sixteen, when he wrote essays for the journal of the Buddhist Lodge in London, he developed a reputation over the next forty years as a foremost interpreter of Eastern philosophies for the West, eventually developing an audience of millions who were enriched through his books, tape recordings, radio and television appearances, and public lectures. He became widely recognized for his Zen writings and for *The Book: On the Taboo Against Knowing Who You Are.*

In all, Watts wrote more than twenty-five books and recorded hundreds of lectures and seminars, all building toward a personal philosophy he shared with honesty and joy with his readers and listeners throughout the world. His overall works have presented a model of individuality and self-expression that can be matched by few philosophers.

Watts came to the United States in 1938, and earned a Master's Degree in Theology from Seabury-Western Theological Seminary. He was Episcopal Chaplain at Northwestern University during World War II, and held fellowships from Harvard University and the Bollingen Foundation. He became professor and dean of the American Academy of Asian Studies in San Francisco and lectured and traveled widely.

He died in 1973 at his home in northern California, survived by his second wife and seven children. A complete list of his books and tapes may be found at www.alanwatts.com.

The book you have just read was created
from the Alan Watts Electronic University
audio tape archive, a vast library of recordings
of his public lectures and seminars.
The archive is the source of Alan Watts'
audio collections, new publications,
and ongoing public radio programs.

For information about ordering
Alan Watts audio collections,
go to www.alanwatts.com
on the Internet, or write or call:

Electronic University
Post Office Box 2309
San Anselmo, CA 94979

Phone: (800) 969-2887
Catalog request: Ext. 2
Ordering: Ext. 3
E-mail: watts@alanwatts.com